Longneedle

Longneedle

Anne Marshall Runyon

ISBN 978-0-86526-500-4

All the illustrations in this book were created by Anne Marshall Runyon and reproduced with permission of the artist.

Illustration on page 14 is shown courtesy of the Nature Conservancy. Julie H. Moore, 2001, *Managing the Forest and the Trees, A Private Landowner's Guide to Conservation Management of Longleaf Pine*, p. 37. The Nature Conservancy, LA Field Office, Baton Rouge.

Special thanks to Mathew Waehner, Photographer, Collections Management Branch, North Carolina State Archives for photographing Ms. Runyon's artwork.

The interior typeface is Yana and the display typeface is Renata. Both fonts are designed by Laura Worthington and distributed through Adobe.

Printed in the United States of America by Jostens. Print management by Martin Book Management.

Distributed by the University of North Carolina Press, Inc.
www.uncpress.org

True Tales for Young Readers

No. 1 *The Life and Times of Asheville's Thomas Wolfe*
Jennifer S. Prince (2016)

No. 2 *We Who Believe in Freedom: The Life and Times of Ella Baker*
Lea E. Williams (2017)

No. 3 *Longneedle*
Anne Marshall Runyon (2020)

Contents

Dear Readers,

This book was inspired by my work and friendship with Lawrence S. Earley, author of *Looking for Longleaf: The Fall and Rise of an American Forest.* The work sent me exploring our beautiful longleaf pine forests, and Larry's friendship encouraged my desire to write a children's book about one longleaf pine.

I am privileged to work in North Carolina with many knowledgeable and enthusiastic educators, writers, botanists, biologists and fellow artists. My work as a natural science illustrator would be impossible without them. Two extraordinary naturalists with deep knowledge of longleaf pine habitats, Julie Moore, a botanist, and Jeffrey Beane, a herpetologist, have patiently taught and shared photos and good times with me over the years. My dear friend, Consie Powell, author and illustrator of beautiful children's books, invited me to join her children's book writers' group, now called Triangle Circle. I cherish the years of learning and fellowship these friends give.

In 2003, I received a United Arts Grant for my longleaf story, enabling me to attend the Society of Children's Book Writers and Illustrators-Carolinas Fall Conference. There I had the opportunity to have an early draft of my manuscript reviewed and critiqued by a publisher's representative.

Recently, a writing class with Susie Wilde honed my story, and as always, my husband, Rick Peifer, and our son, Nate Peifer, have read, re-read, commented on, and encouraged this project.

I am grateful to Michael Hill, and his colleagues at the North Carolina Office of Archives and History, for their patient help, and for publishing my story in their True Tales for Young Readers series.

Warm Regards,

Anne Marshall Runyon

This story was inspired by an old longleaf pine in North Carolina's Coastal Plain. Riddled with woodpecker holes, the dead tree lay decaying among living longleaf pines where red-cockaded woodpeckers maintained an active cluster in the forest. Longneedle is referred to as "she" rather than "it." Our language lacks a pronoun for a being–like a pine tree–that is both male and female at the same time.

1
Out of the Ashes

In the year of 1696, a winged pine seed helicopters to the forest floor, takes root in the sandy soil, and sprouts six green needles. More needles emerge as the longleaf pine seedling grows for two years, nestled in the wiregrass beneath a four-hundred year old tree.

The sky darkens as an early spring storm rumbles closer. Crack! Lightning zaps the top of the old pine tree. A deep gash burns all the way down her thick trunk and the wiregrass below bursts into flames, scorching the pine seedling's needles.

Sparks ignite during the evening. A low fire dances across the hills, blazing the pine straw under the widely spaced trees. The fire burns the grasses, flowers, and shrubs, but thick bark protects the tall longleaf pines. A scarlet snake burrows deep inside his pine stump. Flying squirrels sail between the trees and land, scrambling to safety, high above the flames inside the nest cavities of turkey oaks.

Thunder growls. Raindrops hiss in the flames, splattering the ashy soil. Smoke swirls away from the charred plants. The rain cools the seedling as the fire sizzles down the hillside and dies out before dawn.

Days later, the little pine's scorched needles drop to the ground, exposing a tiny, white tip of her stem–her growing bud. Longneedle survived her first fire!

Each night after the fire, Longneedle drinks water, enriched with ashes and nutrients, to feed her growing bud. Sharp needles poke through the silvery scales that protected her bud during the fire. Animals that fled the fire return to the area.

A week after the fire, a gray fox rests beside singed Longneedle. A six-lined racerunner peeks out of an animal burrow. The fire burned most of the small trees and shrubs growing in the sandy soil of the longleaf forest. Many of the plants, such as turkey oak and blueberry, will regrow. The fire, however, kills most of the young loblolly pines. This is good news for Longneedle! Loblolly pine trees grow quickly, and if they survived the fire, they would shade and stunt the growth of the longleaf pine seedling. Longneedle is a true fire pine, thriving where frequent fires clear away competing trees, creating an open, grassy forest floor.

Bright blades of grass and tender flower tips emerge from the ashes. More of the animals that fled the fire return. A southern hog-nosed snake winds its way toward pinelands star grass. By summer, a colorful meadow surrounds Longneedle. Stimulated by the spring fire, the wiregrass blooms and turns golden in the fall. Longneedle maintains her evergreen color through the seasons.

2
Underground Connections

Longneedle's tap root reaches deep and holds her fast in the sandy, mineral-laden soil of the old growth longleaf pineland. Led by sensitive root tips, the pine seedling's lateral roots radiate outward. Longneedle grips the ground, and her roots tickle the tiny seed-like spores of a fungus, called **amanita** (am`-ah -ne`-tah), resting dormant in the soil. Awakened, the spores fuse with the roots and absorb their sweet sap.

The amanitas wrap around Longneedle's roots and send **hyphae** (hi'-fay) threads throughout the soil. The hyphae absorb water, minerals, and other nutrients. They share food with Longneedle, their host tree, in exchange for her sugary sap. The fungi and the trees help each other survive in a landscape shaped by fire.

Amanita is a **mycorrhizal** (mi`-co -ri`-zal) fungus, a special fungus that forms a partnership with longleaf pine roots. Amanita's hyphae touch and fuse with other amanita hyphae which are attached to the roots of nearby trees. After a rain shower, the amanitas sprout pale mushrooms on the forest floor. The mushrooms open their umbrella-like caps, exposing a petticoat of gills loaded with tiny spores. Breezes scatter the ripe spores across the forest and they settle into the soil, waiting to connect with other pine tree roots.

Two snails and a mantleslug feast on amanita's gills and swallow spores along with the tender flesh. A red-bellied snake hunts the mantleslug and snails. All of these animals spread amanita's spores in their feces as they travel across the forest floor.

Anne Runyon

There are many fungi in longleaf pine forests. Not all fungi that live with trees form these helpful partnerships with their host tree. Many simply eat from their host without giving anything in return. These fungi are called wood-rotters. Honey mushrooms and red-heart fungi are wood-rotters that lurk in Longneedle's forest.

Honey mushrooms are one of box turtles favorite foods to eat.

Another beneficial mycorrhizal partner of Longneedle is **rhyzopogon** (ri-zo-po'-gon), and it lives underground, safe from fire. The fruits of a rhyzopogon ripen underground. Fox squirrels dig them up, eat them, and later spread the fungal spores throughout the forest in their droppings.

Scientists discovered that "mother trees" in old-growth forests like Longneedle's, send nutrients and chemical messages to their younger relatives through underground mycorrhizal connections. For example, a tree attacked by insects may produce repellent chemicals in its leaves and use its underground connections to stimulate other trees to do the same.

Longneedle, rhyzopogon, and the amanitas are joined with the ancient longleaf pine forest community, connected and nurtured for thousands of years by vast underground networks of tree roots and fungi. The soil under Longneedle pulses with constant exchanges of water, nutrients, and chemicals flowing between the pine trees and fungi.

3

Wetland Neighbors

Longneedle grows deep roots in dry, sandy soil on the side of a broad hill in the Sandhills region of the Coastal Plain. At the top of the hill is an ephemeral, or temporary, pond. Water collects in the ephemeral pond during the cooler rainy season and dries up during the hot summer. Fish cannot survive in an ephemeral pond.

Amphibians such as the gopher frog and tiger salamander use the ephemeral ponds to breed and lay their eggs during winter. The aquatic larvae hatch, grow, mature into adults, and leave the ephemeral pond before it dries up.

Farther down the hillside from Longneedle, the sand rests on a dense clay layer that holds water close to the surface. The soil is always moist, and a wetland community called a **seep** flourishes there. Carnivorous pitcher plants, meadow beauties, cinnamon ferns, toothache grass, lilies, and orchids crowd together with many other plants in the damp moss. Mud salamanders also live there.

A pine woods treefrog hunts for insects on tall yellow pitcher plants, and a shrew searches for snails and insects. Fire-dependent pond pines thrive in the seep.

Unlike loblolly pines, pond pines are able to heal themselves by growing new needles and branches after being burned. Fire stimulates their cones to open and drop seeds.

Further down from the seep, a small stream emerges with a burble and meanders through Longneedle's forest, eventually joining a river that flows toward the Atlantic Ocean. Along the stream, longleaf pine trees give way to pond pines, loblolly pines, red maples, black gums, and sweetbay magnolias, as well as a dense understory of gallberries, red bays, switch canes, and vines.

A star-nosed mole burrows in the moist soil under the pond pines.

"Queeeenk!" a green treefrogs calls from the water's edge in spring. Many animals that forage around Longneedle find shelter in these wetlands. During summer, Palamedes swallowtail butterflies lay their eggs on red bay plants. Warblers nest in the cane, and at dusk, big-eared bats hunt for insects in tangled vines and leaves that hang over the water.

Deer, opossums, raccoons, weasels, wolves, and foxes find water, food, and shelter in the streamside forest. Black bears follow the streams, eating tender greens, insect larvae, and berries. Beavers build dams along the stream and create new wetlands in the dry pinelands.

4

People in the Pines

Longneedle's pine forest in the North Carolina Sandhills are part of an ancient longleaf forest ecosystem that spreads across the entire Coastal Plain of the southeastern United States. Near the Atlantic Ocean, the longleaf pine flatwoods and grassy savannas grow next to tangled evergreen pocosins. In the swampy pocosins, pond pines replace the longleaf pines as the dominant tree.

Pocosins are naturally occurring freshwater evergreen shrub bogs, or wetlands, found along the Atlantic coastal plain of the United States, from southern Virginia to northern Florida. An example of a pocosin is on the left side of the illustration, and the right side of the illustration is an example of a savanna.

Centuries before Europeans and Africans arrived, American Indians lived in the Coastal Plains with a rhythm of fire, storm, and seasonal changes. Tuscarora Indians lived among Longneedle's ancestors for generations. They set wiregrass fires to clear land for their small settlements and open up the forest floor for better hunting. The fires also help maintain open, longleaf pine forests.

The Indians gathered herbs, roots, fungi, and berries from these sunny forests. They grew corn, beans, squash, pumpkins, melon, and potatoes. Many fished in the nearby rivers and sounds. The Tuscarora skirmished with other tribes, avenging the death of their warriors by killing or capturing enemy warriors.

After European colonists arrived, the Indians traded deerskins and enemy captives as slaves to the colonists in exchange for useful new tools such as guns, ammunition, and a variety of metal wares. The European and African newcomers also brought deadly new diseases, such as smallpox and

measles to the Indians, and sadly, many died. The colonists claimed the pinelands, clearing away ancient forests to build roads, forts, towns, and fields.

In 1696, as Longneedle sprouts, England requests the American colonies to supply naval stores for the Royal Navy. Naval stores are forest products used in shipbuilding such as timber, tar, pitch, turpentine, and rosin. Harvesting the vast longleaf pine forests covering the Coastal Plain was profitable for both England and the American colonies.

Tall pines were cut into timbers for masts, spars, and planking. Oak timbers were used to build sturdy hulls. Dead pine wood contained resin and was burned to produce tar. Tar was then boiled to make pitch. Resin collected from living pines was distilled into turpentine and rosin.

5
Rising Above the Flames

In 1704 Longneedle's tap root grows deeper and her mycorrhizal connections expand. She also sprouts more needles from the tip of her stem. Longneedle continues to grow slowly and protects her fragile bud. Her needles regrow quickly after another spring fire crackles under the pines. Longneedle is an eight-year-old tree, but she resembles a clump of evergreen grass.

During Longneedle's twelfth winter, a fierce nor'easter wind roars across the forest. The ancient, lightning-scarred longleaf pine tree that towers over Longneedle crashes to the ground. After the storm passes, Longneedle glistens in the sunshine.

Spring rains and warm sun wash over the pinelands. The seedling's green needles harvest the energy of the sun with chlorophyll producing a sugar called glucose that fuels her growth. Longneedle stretches straight up toward the warm, shining sun.

Within two years, Longneedle becomes a six-foot-tall pole with bright green needles bristling all along her skinny trunk.

During late fall, two Tuscarora hunters set fire to the hills. Longneedle is a skinny fourteen-year-old pole. More hunters hide downwind with spears, bows, and arrows ready to slay animals that flee the fire. The Tuscarora feed their families with the meat and use the hides to make clothing. The flames singed Longneedle's thick, flaky bark and bristling green needles, but her growing bud waves high above the fire and the young fire pine again survives.

Each spring, several new buds emerge along Longneedle's stem and form curving branches that resemble tall, white candles..

Longneedle continues to rapidly grow. Green needles crowd along new growth, and birds such as brown-headed nuthatches and red-cockaded woodpeckers probe for hidden insects. As Longneedle grows taller, her lower branches which are shaded, die and break off.

Fire burns across the pinelands every few years, and the shrubby turkey oaks near Longneedle burn to the ground each time. Neighboring turkey oaks located just over the hill from Longneedle escape the Tuscarora's fire and grow into small trees. Over time, they also become tall enough to resist later fires and form a beautiful oak grove. Fox squirrels, deer, and turkeys enjoy eating the acorns.

Longneedle's graceful branches curve outward and upward, holding the green needles safe above the dancing flames. The fire pine grows taller and her bark thickens.

6
Cones and Seeds, Plenty for All

1710 Longneedle is still a six-foot-tall skinny pine growing in the Sandhills. Swiss and German colonists build the town of New Bern at the mouth of the Neuse River, and the Tuscarora Indians who live south of the new town join together under Chief Hancock and battle to regain their territories.

1711 The Tuscarora lost the war and also their homelands to the colonists. After the Tuscarora War, more colonial settlers moved westward across the Coastal Plains. These events forever changed the longleaf forest landscape.

1727 By the time Longneedle first blooms, valuable naval stores, tar and pitch, are produced from the open longleaf pine forests spreading across the Coastal Plains in the Carolinas. Colonists established a port at Brunswick on the Cape Fear River in North Carolina. The naval stores were rafted down the river in barrels and loaded onto large ships at Brunswick. The ships sailed north to Philadelphia, New York, and Boston where merchants exported the barrels across the Atlantic to England. These commodities were the backbone of the colonial economy, as England needed tar and pitch for the Royal Navy, and also to sell to other countries.

The Carolina parakeet (*right*) is an extinct parrot species and the only parrot species native to the eastern United States.

Making tar and pitch is very difficult work and mostly done by enslaved people. Dead longleaf pine wood, heavy with resin, is gathered and burned inside earthen kilns. Tar oozes out from the bottom of the hot kiln, leaving a pile of charcoal inside.

Tar boiled in huge kettles produces sticky pitch. The tar is used to strengthen and preserve a sailing ship's rigging, which is made of rope. Pitch coats a ship's hull, sealing out the sea water and repelling wood-boring mollusks.

In 1727, thirty-one-year-old Longneedle is almost fifty feet tall when she sprouts clusters of purple, male flowers along her branches.

Male longleaf flowers begin to grow in late winter-early spring. The flowers grow up to three inches long and turn rosy pink as they fill with pollen. In early spring, nearly all the mature longleaf pine flowers release clouds of dry, yellow pollen.

Longneedle's tiny female flowers emerge just behind the growing tips of her branches. When just sprouting, female longleaf pine flowers are soft and pink.

The twin female flowers grow upward and are fertilized when breezes dust everything with yellow pollen.

Once fertilized, the flowers develop into stiff cones as they twist down, growing long and green.

For two years the pinecones fatten as the seeds ripen, and the cones turn brown. A hungry fox squirrel cuts off a large, green cone and drops it to the ground. He scampers down the pine tree, picks up the cone, and carries it to the stump where he feasts on the seeds.

During the summer of 1728 a lightning fire chars the forest floor and clears it of debris. In autumn, Longneedle's ripe brown cones open. Winged seeds helicopter downward. Some seeds are gobbled up by birds, mammals, and ants. Hungry bob-white quail scratch for them under the wiregrass and autumn flowers. A pine snake slides out from her den inside a pine stump and catches a mouse nibbling on the pine seeds.

Seeds that land on open ground rapidly thrust tiny roots into the earth seeking food, water, and fungal partners. Insects eat some seeds, but many others survive and sprout into seedlings around Longneedle.

No Fire, No Seedlings... The Story of a Longleaf Pine

In February the longleaf pine begins to flower. Its male catkins release clouds of yellow pollen. Spring breezes carry the pollen to tiny female flowers perched along the branches. Two years pass as the fertilized flowers mature into huge pine coves filled with large seeds. During the second summer, a small lightning fire burns the forest clear.

In late October, the cones slowly open and seeds drift downward landing near the parent tree. Many seeds are eaten, as they are nutritious food, and some seeds never reach the ground. But one seed lands on open soil, germinates, and sends tiny roots into the sandy soil. Ashes from the summer fire and winter rains nourish the little seedling. A baby longleaf pine begins to grow.

A seed develops in winter and spring...

by summer, a fire resistant seedling grows.

7

A Profitable Commodity

Scottish Highlanders settle in the Sandhill region during the mid-1700s and clear trees to create roads, farms, and towns. They also cut the longleaf pine forests to produce naval stores and timber. Transporting these resources through the sandy hills to distant ports is difficult and slow work.

Fortunately, Longneedle's hill is left undisturbed, however, healthy underground connections between the forest tree roots and the mycorrhizal fungi are damaged by the settlers. Throughout the eighteenth century, Longneedle widens her trunk and thickens her bark. As her older needles fall, new needles emerge. Every six or seven years, Longneedle produces a bumper crop of cones. As Longneedle continues to mature, the American colonies form, fight against England, and win independence in 1776 to become the United States of America.

Stages of longleaf pine growth from seedling to fallen log.

Forest exploitation for naval stores in North Carolina booms during the nineteenth century. Merchants build railroads into the longleaf forests throughout the Coastal Plain, including Longneedle's Sandhills region. Railroads make transporting the heavy timbers and barrels of tar, pitch, and turpentine through the sandy hills profitable.

Landowners send workers, mostly slaves, throughout the longleaf forests to tap the living pines for their fragrant resin, which is collected and ladled into barrels. Mules pull wooden carts loaded with heavy barrels of pine resin to stills. The resin is distilled into liquid spirits of turpentine and hard rosin. The two pungent pine products are used to make paint, wax, lamp fuel, ink, rubber, soap, and medicine. Tacky rosin rubbed on a violin's bow makes the strings sing.

Massive four-hundred-year-old longleaf pine trees are felled for their high-grade wood and shipped by rail to sawmills. The valuable timber is used for shipbuilding and construction, making strong masts, sturdy beams and beautiful, wide floorboards. Schooners transport barrels of naval stores from North Carolina's Cape Fear River to New England ports.

Tar becomes one of North Carolina's most profitable commodities, earning North Carolinians the somewhat derogatory nickname "Tar Heels." During the Civil War, North Carolina's Confederate troops, however, embrace the nickname "Tar Heels" because soldiers held their ground in battle, as if their boots were sticky with tar.

By the end of the nineteenth century, most of the old growth longleaf pines growing throughout the Coastal Plain of North Carolina are cut down. Tobacco and other crops are planted where longleaf pines once grew.

Towns, farms, and roads stop lightning fires that once burned freely across the land. Longleaf pine cannot regrow without the fires. Fast-growing loblolly pines mixed with hardwoods like oak, hickory, sweet gum, and maple replace the original fire-dependent longleaf forests in North Carolina.

8

In the Heart of the Tree

A storm tears off a living limb in the late summer of 1896 and a ragged hole is left in Longneedle's protective bark. Red heart fungus from a nearby longleaf pine releases spores into the air. The spores drift and land on the hole before Longneedle can seal off the wound with resin. The wood rotting fungus does not kill the tree but slowly softens her dense inner heartwood.

During WWI, Fort Bragg military base is established in the Sandhills near Southern Pines. The explosives tested and the fires burned maintain the longleaf pines and other fire dependent species around the base. WWI also increases the demand for lumber, and many longleaf pines are timbered.

To help the country recover from the Great Depression, as part of the New Deal, the Croatan National Forest is established in 1936 on 50,000 acres near New Bern. The United States Forest Service employs the Civilian Conservation Corps (CCC) to plant loblolly pine plantations where longleaf pine forest once grow.

The U.S. Forest Service uses Smokey Bear ads to create awareness of forest fire prevention across the United States. The campaign increases the planting of loblolly plantations but limits longleaf pine regeneration on public lands. Many farmers burn their pine forests to maintain wiregrass and open up woodland for their sheep and cattle to graze. In the Sandhills, seeds from Longneedle continue to sprout after fire clears the forest floor.

Longneedle is a grand two-hundred-fifty-year-old tree in 1946, topped with a crown of long twisting branches. The red heart fungus slowly grows inside of her. It matures and pushes a corky fruiting body through the bark under one of Longneedle's branches.

A male red-cockaded woodpecker lands on Longneedle's sturdy trunk. The small bird taps and listens. From the sound of the taps, the woodpecker senses that Longneedle's soft heartwood is easy to excavate.

Over two years the woodpecker chips through the tough living layers of Longneedle's trunk and digs a deep nest hole inside the rotted heartwood. He also drills shallow pits around his entrance hole. Wounded Longneedle oozes sticky resin down the trunk, trying to seal the small pits. The bird keeps the pits open because the flowing resin prevents rat snakes and ants from climbing up and bothering his nest.

The red-cockaded woodpecker attracts a female in early spring, and she lays three eggs in the nest cavity. Together, the pair raises their babies as they grow and learn to fly by summer. The three fledglings roost with their parents in the cavity through the winter. In the spring, the young females depart to search for mates. Their brother remains to help raise the next brood while also working on his own nest hole in a nearby pine. After helping his parents for a few years, he is joined by a female. Younger brothers take his place as helpers and add more nest holes in nearby pines.

In 1956, a small cluster of red-cockaded woodpeckers thrive in and around Longneedle. A multi-generational family of longleaf pines shelters an extended woodpecker family. Birds assist in the maintenance of a healthy forest by eating ants, bark beetles, and other insects that could potentially harm the trees.

Anoles, red-cockaded woodpeckers, bobwhite quail, pine elfin butterflies, red-tailed hawks, rat snakes, gray foxes, cottontail rabbits, and bluebirds are among the many animals living within Longneedle's Sandhills pine forest.

9

Fire Pine Hotel

Lightning strikes the top of Longneedle during the summer of 1980, and it deeply scars her trunk. For more than eighty years, red heart fungus rotted her heartwood. Longneedle could not bear the brunt of this injury, and she begins to die.

The following spring, Longneedle's sap fails to rise. Resin stops flowing out of pits drilled around the red-cockaded woodpeckers' nest hole, and they abandon their dying tree in search of other mature longleaf pine trees to make their nests.

Needles gently drop from Longneedle's crown as a pair of bluebirds claim the abandoned nest hole and lay four bright blue eggs inside the tall tree. The bluebird family hunts for grasshoppers and caterpillars in the grasses and shrubs. The dead pine is filled with bird life again as the bluebirds return to nest for several years.

One spring, a pair of pileated woodpeckers enlarge the old red-cockaded nest hole before the bluebirds return. The new woodpeckers raise three of their young inside the dead tree that spring. These large woodpeckers hammer and tear off slabs of bark searching for wood-boring beetles and grubs in the pines, the turkey oak grove, and the streamside forest. They excavate a new nest hole above their first one. As years go by, red-headed and red-bellied woodpeckers take their turns hollowing more cavities in the dead tree.

A flying squirrel moves into one of the woodpecker holes. She nurses her six helpless babies inside Longneedle for about seven weeks. The young squirrels then join their mother foraging for seeds, nuts, berries, insects, and bird eggs. They glide across the forest at night.

Longneedle continues to shed her bark and limbs, becoming a white snag in the shimmering green forest.

10

Continuity of Nature

Hurricane Fran roars through the forest in the fall of 1996. Longneedle, having stood for three-hundred years, crashes to the ground, crushing blueberries and turkey oaks.

During the spring of 1997, a male, eastern fence lizard perches on the fallen log, bobbing his head and blue throat patches to attract a female. She digs a burrow and lays her eggs under Longneedle.

Slowly the old tree decays, enriching the soil. Two of Longneedle's descendants nestle beside her. They glisten in the sunlight, and a new generation of longleaf pines begins to grow straight, reaching for the sun.

The Old North State

Here's to the land of the long leaf pine,

The summer land where the sun doth shine,

Where the weak grow strong and the strong grow great,

Here's to "Down Home," the Old North State!"

North Carolina Conservation Efforts

1963 "Weymouth" in Southern Pines was the home of novelist James Boyd and his wife, Katherine. After James's death, Katherine donated 403 acres of her family's land to the state of North Carolina, establishing the Weymouth Woods Nature Preserve. Longleaf pine forests remain protected there.

1973 The Endangered Species Act became federal law. Studies of the endangered red-cockaded woodpeckers' habitat helped establish the practice of prescribed burning to limit understory tree growth in longleaf forests.

1976 The North Carolina Natural Heritage Program was established to inventory and support conservation of rare plants and animals that are unique to North Carolina.

1977 The state of North Carolina purchased the Boyd Timber Tract, an old-growth Longleaf pine forest, for Weymouth Woods Sandhills Nature Preserve. The oldest living longleaf pine–more than four-hundred-sixty years old–lives there. Her trunk is thick, gnarled, and sports a crown of twisted branches.

1977 The Federal Paper Board Company donated 13,850 acres of the Green Swamp, a National Natural Landmark, to a newly established North Carolina chapter of the Nature Conservancy. The carnivorous Venus flytrap and other rare plants and animals thrive in longleaf pine savannas.

1985 Botanist Joan Walker documented the amazing plant diversity in the ground cover of the Green Swamp's wiregrass savannas. These numbers rivaled the diversity within tropical rainforests. The Nature Conservancy and other conservation groups became more interested in restoring longleaf pine forests, and broadened their views to include the whole forest, and not just the trees.

1995 The Longleaf Alliance, a non-profit organization in Alabama, formed as an information clearing house for longleaf pine growers throughout the longleaf range from Virginia to Texas.

2004 *Looking for Longleaf: The Fall and Rise of an American Forest* by Lawrence S. Earley was published by the University of North Carolina Press.

Today The land continues to be slashed and separated by roads, railroads, farms, towns, and cities. Ancient underground mycorrhizal connections are broken. Fires no longer burn freely and frequently across the Coastal Plains. Without fire, the longleaf pines, wiregrass meadows, pitcher plants, red-cockaded woodpeckers, and the other amazing fire-dependent species that evolved here are dwindling. Longleaf pine supporters–including state and federal agencies, private groups, and individual landowners–have joined efforts to regenerate North Carolina's longleaf pinelands. They work to create larger forests by connecting existing ones, making the land easier to burn successfully. Prescribed and controlled burns are used to restore open pine forests and preserve their unique biodiversity. Perhaps in another three centuries, old growth longleaf pine forests, like the one where Longneedle sprouted, may once again flourish in North Carolina.

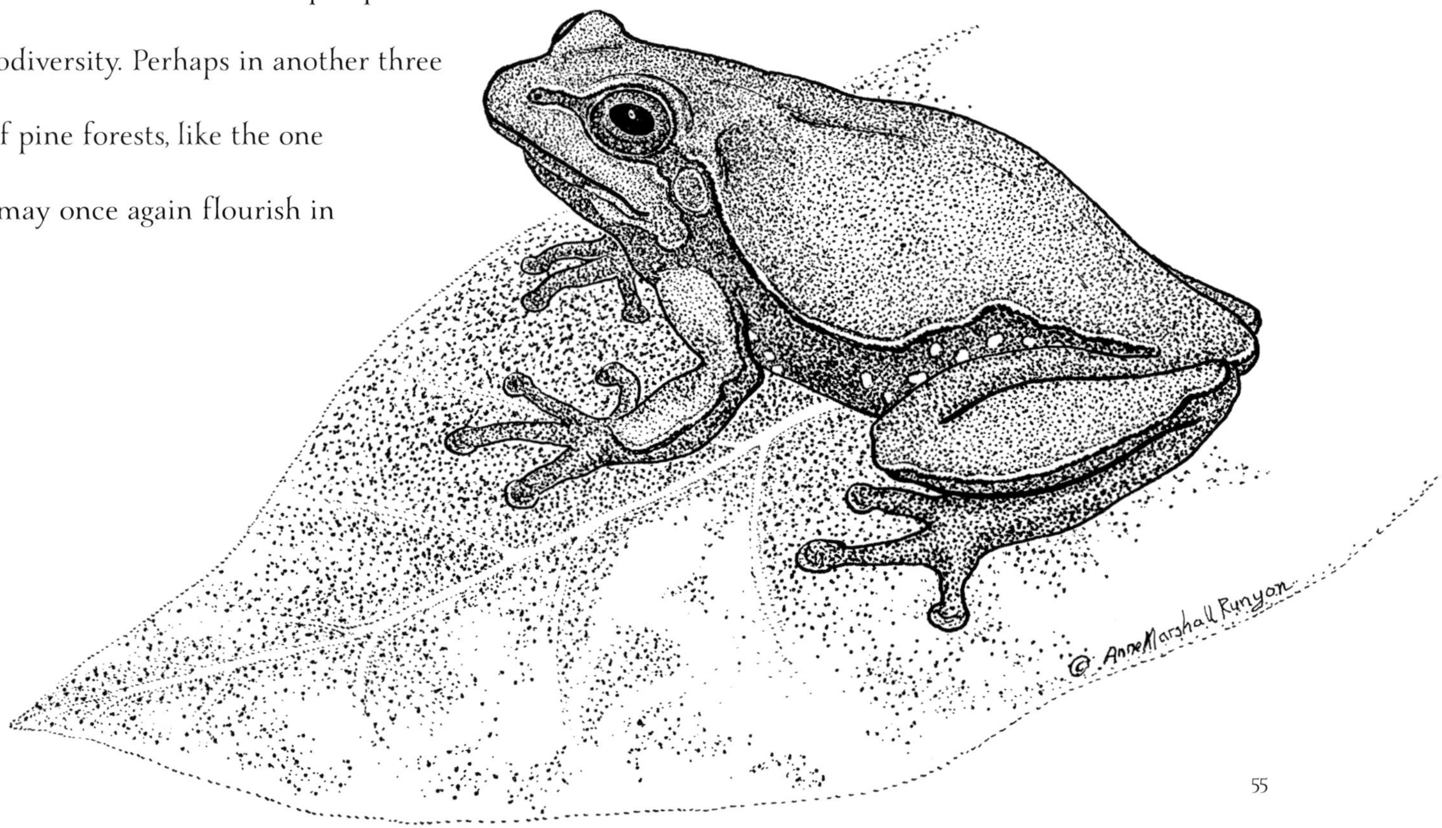

Resources about Longleaf Forests and Naval Stores in North Carolina

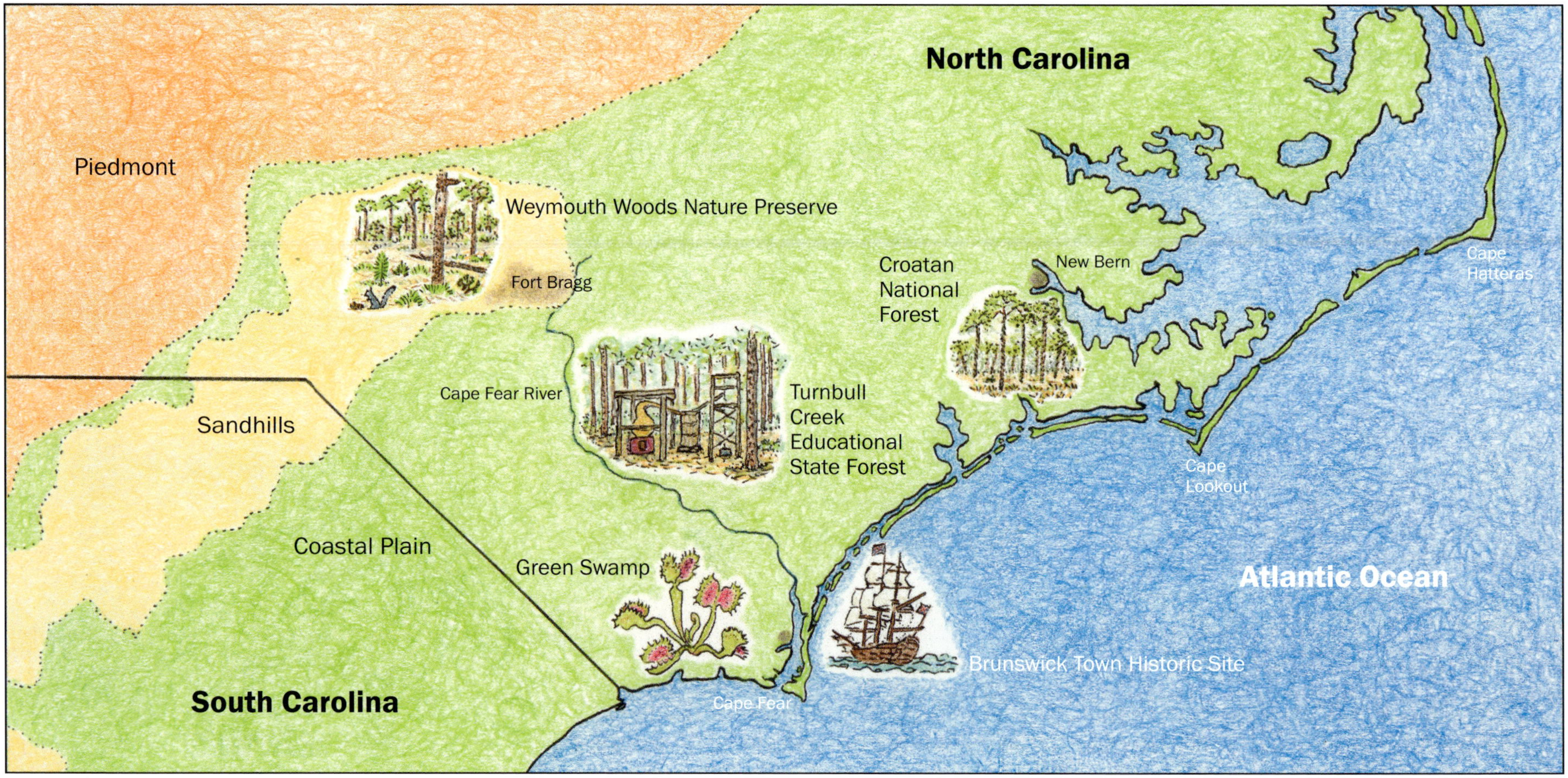

Sites

Weymouth Woods Sandhills Nature Preserve
1024 N. Fort Bragg Road
Southern Pines, NC 28387
https://www.ncparks.gov/weymouth-woods-sandhills-nature-preserve

Weymouth Woods Nature Preserve is a 915-acre state park featuring Sandhills longleaf pine forests, like Longneedle's forest. Each April, the park hosts a birthday party celebrating their oldest living longleaf pine with fun and educational activities in the forest.

The Nature Conservancy's Green Swamp
673 Green Swamp Road, NW
Supply, NC 28462
https://www.nature.org/en-us/get-involved/how-to-help/places-we-protect/green-swamp-preserve/

The Green Swamp contains some of the country's finest examples of longleaf pine savannas. The Nature Conservancy's many management activities at the Green Swamp include controlled burning and restoring pine plantations to longleaf pine savannas.

The Croatan National Forest
141 E. Fisher Avenue
New Bern, NC 28560
https://www.visitnc.com/listing/6xMx/croatan-national-forest

This coastal National Forest contains 159,000 acres of estuary, hardwood forest, longleaf pine, and pocosin. Recreation areas are available for camping, picnicking, swimming, canoeing, hiking, and wildlife observation.

Brunswick Town/ Fort Anderson Historic Site
8884 St. Philip's Road SE
Winnabow, NC 28479
https://historicsites.nc.gov/all-sites/brunswick-town-fort-anderson

A major pre-Revolutionary port on North Carolina's Cape Fear River, Brunswick was razed by British troops in 1776 and never rebuilt. During the Civil War, Fort Anderson was constructed atop the old village site, and served as part of the Cape Fear River defenses below Wilmington before the fall of the Confederacy. Colonial foundations dot the present-day tour trail, which crosses the earthworks of the Confederate fort.

Turnbull Creek Educational State Forest
4803 Sweet Home Church Road
Elizabethtown, NC 28337
https://www.ncesf.org/turnbull.html

Turnbull Creek Educational State Forest is a 890-acre North Carolina State Forest in Elizabethtown, North Carolina. It is the only educational state forest (ESF) located in North Carolina's Coastal Plain.

Books

Looking for Longleaf: The Fall and Rise of an American Forest
Lawrence S. Earley
The University of North Carolina Press, Chapel Hill, 2004

Longleaf, Far as The Eye Can See: A New Vision of North America's Richest Forest
Bill Finch, Beth Maynor Young, Rhett Johnson & John C. Hall
University of North Carolina Press, Chapel Hill, 2012

The Hidden Life of Trees-What They Feel, How They Communicate-Discoveries from a Secret World
Peter Wohlleben
(English Translation)
Greystone Books Ltd.
David Suzuki Institute, 2016

Videos

"Secrets of the Longleaf Pine"
Red Sky Productions
Atlanta, GA
www.longleafpine.org

"Longleaf: The Heart of Pine"
Rex Jones
University of Mississippi
Southern Documentary Project
www.southdocs.org/project/longleaf

Anne Runyon was born in Washington, D.C. Summers spent on Ocracoke Island, N.C. nurtured her love of the natural world. Her family inspired her to be an artist. She earned her BA in studio art from Carleton College and studied design and children's literature in the Kerlan Collection while earning her MA from the University of Minnesota. She and her husband moved to North Carolina in 1982, where their son was born and grew up.

Anne is a freelance illustrator and author. She works on paper with ink, watercolor, and colored pencil creating illustrations for environmental publications and exhibits. She writes and illustrates children's books, creates woodcut prints, and designs paper sculpture craft activities.

North Carolina Wild Places–A Closer Look, edited by Lawrence S. Earley, is illustrated with her detailed habitat drawings. Ink and watercolor paintings enrich Anne's picture book, *The Sheltering Cedar*. *Longneedle* is a song of praise for the beautiful longleaf pine forests.

©Anne Runyon